Ben's birthday mystery

Keith Gaines

Nelson

'It will soon be your birthday,' said Ben's Mum.
'Do you want to have a party?'
'I'm not sure,' said Ben.
'Do you think I'm getting too old for a birthday party?'
'Not at all!' said his Mum.
She put her arm around Ben.
'You're still my little boy.'

Ben's Mum went on talking.
'You must have some of your friends round and you can have a lovely birthday party.'
'Oh, Mum. Don't be silly!' said Ben.
'I'm not a little boy any longer.
I'm getting bigger and bigger all the time!'
Ben sat down.

'I'd like a party,' said Ben,
'but I don't really want the sort of children's party where we have jelly and ice-cream and cake. That sort of party is really for little kids.'
'Well, what sort of party do you want?' said his Mum.
'I don't really know,' said Ben.
Ben's Dad came in.
'Hello,' said Ben's Mum.
'Tea will be ready in five minutes.'
'Are you going to the gym tomorrow?' Ben asked his Dad.
Every Saturday, Ben's Dad went to a gym.
He did weight training there.
Sometimes Ben went with him.
'Well,' said Ben's Dad,
'there's a big new gym that has just opened.
It's not far away.
I thought I'd have a look at it and see if it's any good.
It's called something like *Sport for all the Family*, or *The Sports Hall*.
Anyway, I know where it is.
Do you want to come?'
'OK!' said Ben.

On Saturday morning, Ben and his Dad went to the new gym.
It was called *Sports for All*.
'Well, I was close,' said Ben's Dad.
'I knew it was something like that,' he laughed as he looked at the big sign outside.

They went through the front door.
'Hello,' said a lady.
'Have you been to *Sports for All* before?'
'No,' said Ben's Dad.
'This is the first time we've been here.
We came to look at the gym and
to see if we could do weight training.'
'We have a big gym that all the family can use,'
said the lady.
'That's where you go for weight training.
We also have a climbing wall in the gym.
The gym is next to the big sports hall.'

The lady went on,
'At the other end of the sports hall is the water gym,
where you can swim, you can do diving, or
you can just splash around.
You can have a cup of tea in the room upstairs.
You can get food there, too.'

'Well,' said Ben's Dad.
'What shall we do?'
'Why don't we do some weight training, and
then go for a swim?' said Ben.
'That sounds OK to me,' said his Dad.
'Let's get started!'
'Through here, please,' said the lady.

Ben and his Dad put on their gym clothes.
'Wow! Look at that!'
said Ben, as they went into the gym.
'There's someone half-way up that wall!'
'That must be the climbing wall,' said his Dad.
'And look at that trampoline. That's a big one, isn't it?
Look, there's the weight training stuff over there.'

Ben and his Dad did their weight training.
Ben kept looking at the climbing wall.
'It looks really difficult,' thought Ben.
'But it looks as if it might be great fun.'
'Let's go and have a swim now,' said his Dad.

Ben went to dip his foot into the water.
'What are you waiting for?' asked his Dad.
'I don't like it when I first go in the water,' said Ben.
'It's OK when you're in the water, but
it's very cold when you first get in.'
'Let me help,'
said his Dad and he gave Ben a big push.

Splash!
Ben fell into the water and
his Dad went diving in after him.
'Hey!' shouted Ben.
'It's really warm.'
Ben had a long swim and
he splashed around in
the water with his Dad.
Suddenly, Ben's Dad grabbed his arm.

'Look up there,' said Ben's Dad.
'That must be the tea room.
It looks as if someone is having a party.
Your mother said that you were
worried about your birthday.
Well, why don't we have your birthday party here?
You could get a few of your friends to come.
We could all have a swim, and then we could
have a party, like those people.'
'Hey,' said Ben, 'that would be great!'

On their way out, Ben's Dad asked the lady about
having a birthday party at *Sports for All*.
'Yes,' said the lady.
'You can go for a swim at any time, and
you can have a small birthday party upstairs.
If you want to, you can book the gym so that
only you and your friends can use it.
Would you like to book it for
two hours from half-past-six?'
'Yes, please,' said Ben's Dad. 'That would be great.
I think Ben will have a birthday he'll
remember for years.'

Two weeks later it was Ben's birthday.
When Ben came downstairs that morning,
his Mum and Dad said,
'Happy birthday, Ben!
There is something for you on the table.'
Ben looked at the table.
There was a letter on it.
It said '*Happy birthday to Ben*' on the front.
Ben opened the letter.

The letter said,

Look on the poster that's up on the wall,
Or pick up a letter from inside the hall.
Find the next one, but be sure you don't fall!
Look on the bars or look on the ball.
There's something for you at Sports for All!
Have a lovely birthday,
from Mum and Dad. xxx

'What's this?' said Ben.
'That's your birthday surprise from me and Mum,' said his Dad.
'It's something we've bought you for your birthday. It's at *Sports for All* but you have to find it after your party.'

Just then, someone banged on the door.
It was Wing Chan.
'Happy birthday, Ben,' he said. 'This is for you.
I can't stay. I have to go shopping with my Mum.'
'Was that your new friend, Chow Wing Chan?'
asked Ben's Dad.
'Yes,' said Ben. 'He comes from Hong Kong.
He's only been living in this country for a few months.
He's coming to the party.'

Later that day, Ben's Mum and Dad took
Ben, Rocky, Jamila, Wing Chan, Tony and Tessa to
Sports for All.
'Is Kevin coming?' asked Jamila.
'I asked him, but he's gone on a
shopping trip with his Mum and Dad,' said Ben.
'First, we're all going for a swim,'
Ben's Mum said to him.
'Then we'll have something to eat, and
then you can start looking for your surprise.'

Ben and his friends all went for a swim.
'I can't swim very well,' said Wing Chan.
'There's no danger here,' said Rocky.
'It's not very deep.'
'I was afraid of the water when I couldn't swim,' said Ben.
'Now he loves it,' said Tony.

Ben and his friends had a great time in the water.
As they were playing, Ben's Dad got out of the water.
'Where are you going, Dad?' asked Ben.
'I'm just going to see about something,' said his Dad.
'Stay in here for a few more minutes, and then you can get out and go upstairs for your birthday tea.'

All the children put on their other clothes and went upstairs with Ben's Mum for their party.
'Isn't Dad coming to the party?'
asked Ben, as he helped himself to another crisp.
'He'll be here in a few minutes,' said Ben's Mum.
'He has to see about something first.'

When they had finished eating,
Ben looked at his letter again.
'It says,
"*Look on the poster that's up on the wall,
Or pick up a letter from inside the hall.*"'
'You have to find another letter,' said Ben's Mum.
'I think there was a poster where we
came in downstairs,' said Rocky.
'So I could look downstairs or I could look in the hall,'
said Ben. 'Where shall I go first?'

*Can you help Ben to find his birthday surprise?
If you want Ben to go and look on the poster on
the wall downstairs, go to p 24.
If you want Ben to go and look in the hall, go to p 25.*

'I can't see any letter on the wall,' said Tessa.
'You have to look on the poster,' said Wing Chan.
'Look! There is a letter stuck onto that poster.'
Ben took it down and opened it.
It said,

> There's no surprise stuck on this wall.
> Look in the gym or in the hall!

'Well,' said Ben.
'Shall I go to the hall or shall I go to the gym?'

Where should Ben go now?
If you want Ben to go to the hall, go to p 25.
If you want Ben to go to the gym, go to p 27.

Ben and his friends ran to the hall and
opened the door.
Inside the hall, people were playing football.

A man came up to them.
'You can't come in here,' he said.
'Just a minute. Is your name Ben?'
'Yes,' said Ben.
'Well, I've got this for you,' said the man,
and he gave Ben a letter.
Ben opened the letter.
It said,

Your birthday surprise is not in the hall.
Why don't you look up on the wall?

Go to p 26.

'But what wall should we look on?' said Wing Chan. 'There's a wall there and another one there and another one over there.'
'Your first letter says,
"*Find the next one, but be sure you don't fall!*"' said Rocky.
'What sort of wall could you fall off in here?'
'There's a climbing wall in the gym,' said Ben.
'Let's have a look at that.'

Go to p 27.

'Look!' said Jamila. 'There is the letter.'
'Yes,' said Ben, 'and there's only one way to get it.'
Ben climbed very carefully up the climbing wall.
As soon as he could, he reached out his hand and grabbed the letter.
He dropped it down to his friends.
'Tell me what it says as I climb down,' he shouted.
Tessa caught the letter.
Then she shouted up to Ben,

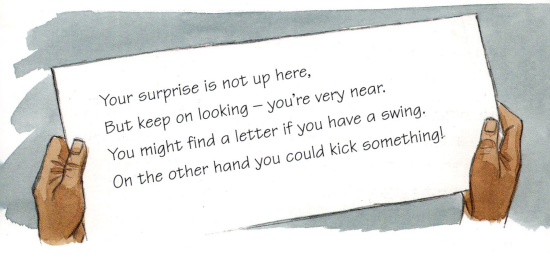

Your surprise is not up here,
But keep on looking – you're very near.
You might find a letter if you have a swing.
On the other hand you could kick something!

'But what could you kick?' said Tony.
'You could kick that football over there,' said Tessa.

Go to p 28.

Ben dropped to the ground.
'Where shall I go next?' he asked.
'I can't see any swings in here,' said Rocky.
'Aren't those bars over there for swinging on?' said Jamila.
'Anyway, your letter said,
"*Look on the bars or look on the ball.*"'

Where should Ben look next?
If you want Ben to look on the ball, go to p 29.
If you want Ben to look on the bars, go to p 30.

Ben looked at the ball.
'You were right,' he said to Tessa.
'There's another letter on it.'
The letter said,

You're nearly there. I think you'd better swing on the bars to find the letter!

'I can't see anything on these bars,' said Jamila.
'It says I have to swing on them,' said Ben.

Go to p 30.

'I've never done this before,' said Ben,
'Oh, well. Here goes!'
Ben grabbed the bars and jumped up.
As he started to swing he saw another
letter, stuck on top of one of the bars.
'There it is,' shouted Ben, and he jumped down.
He reached up and opened the letter.

Go to p 31.

The letter said,

*Your birthday surprise you've already seen!
Look under the little trampoline.*
'I haven't seen anything that could be
a birthday surprise,' said Ben.
'I've only seen gym stuff in here.
What could it be?'

**Do you know what Ben's birthday surprise is?
Find out on p 32.**

Ben crawled under the little trampoline.
There was another letter stuck under it. It said,

> There's nothing more for you to do.
> This trampoline is just for you.

'So this trampoline is my birthday surprise!' said Ben.
'Yes,' said his Dad.
'You won't have to use that old bed any longer.
We thought you'd like a good trampoline for
your birthday.'
'That was a brilliant mystery,' said Ben,
'and a brilliant birthday party.'
'Good,' said his Mum.
'Now, we can use this gym until half-past-eight.
Then we'll take you all home.'
'How do we get the trampoline home?' asked Ben.
His Dad opened a little book and said,
'It took me hours to put the trampoline
together in the sports hall this morning,
but it says in here,
"It is easy to fit your trampoline into a car."
Here, you have the book.
See if you can solve another mystery!'

The end